T0069056

What Was Communism?
A SERIES EDITED BY TARIQ ALI

The theory of Communism as enunciated by Marx and En-
gels in *The Communist Manifesto* spoke the language of freedom,
allied to reason. A freedom from exploitation in conditions
that were being created by the dynamic expansion of capitalism so that 'all that is solid melts into air'. The system was
creating its own grave-diggers. But capitalism survived. It was
the regimes claiming loyalty to the teachings of Marx that
collapsed and reinvented themselves. What went wrong?

This series of books explores the practice of twentieth-
century Communism. Was the collapse inevitable? What
actually happened in different parts of the world? And is
there anything from that experience that can or should be
rehabilitated? Why have so many heaven-stormers become
submissive and gone over to the camp of reaction? With
capitalism mired in a deep crisis, these questions become
relevant once again. Marx's philosophy began to be regarded
as a finely spun web of abstract and lofty arguments, but one
that had failed the test of experience. Perhaps, some argued,
it would have been better if his followers had remained idle
dreamers and refrained from political activity. The
Communist system lasted 70 years and failed only once.
Capitalism has existed for over half a millennium and failed
regularly. Why is one collapse considered the final and the
other episodic? These are some of the questions explored in
a variety of ways by writers from all over the globe, many
living in countries that once considered themselves
Communist states.

back in the ussr

BORIS KAGARLITSKY

LONDON NEW YORK CALCUTTA

Seagull Books 2009

© Boris Kagarlitsky 2009

ISBN-13   978 1 9064 9 727 9

British Library Cataloguing-in-Publication Data
A catalogue record for this book is available
from the British Library

Jacket and book designed by Sunandini Banerjee, Seagull Books
Printed at Rockwel Offset, Calcutta

A strange aspect of the post-Soviet cultural situation in Russia and other former republics of the USSR is that, almost two decades after the disintegration of the old state, they still remain and identify themselves as post-Soviet. Ten years after the fall of Tsarism, nobody in Russia referred to its legacy to explain anything going on in the country. And if the old regime was referred to at all, it was to show the difference from the past.

Not so in the former USSR.

Of course, the difference between the Soviet past and the capitalist present is striking. But this makes the question even more intriguing: why are the new elites referring to the old days to legitimize themselves? Why do commercial advertisements tell you that the product they offer is exactly the same as it used to be in Soviet times? Why, year after year, does the government in Moscow organize impressive celebrations of Victory Day, which invariably remind you of the old Soviet ceremonies?

But, at the same time, legitimizing themselves through continuity with the USSR doesn't make Russian elites less anti-Communist. While the praise of former Soviet glory is one part of the game, propaganda about the horrors of Soviet life is another. TV shows and films with impressive budgets provided by the state are dedicated to Stalinist repressions and the heroic deeds of the White Guards who fought against the Bolsheviks.

You may well say that the Russian propaganda machine is schizophrenic. But the real question is: why is it so?

Right after the demise of the Soviet Union, the situation was different. The new state identified itself as 'the New Russia', which claimed to have very little in common with the previous regime. It proclaimed the 12th of June to be the day of Russian Independence, as if our country had been conquered or occupied by some external force and only in 1991, when the Russian republican parliament (still within the USSR) voted for the 'Declaration of Sovereignty', had this situation ended. Later, the public holiday continued to exist but official propaganda no longer dared to call it 'independence day'; it was transformed into plain 'Russia Day'. Practically speaking, no one wondered why this precise day was chosen.

THE MAKING OF A RULING CLASS

The new commercial elite emerging in Moscow and other cities after the end of the Soviet system quickly became known as 'New Russians'. Soon, there were a slew of jokes about their strange habits and excessively luxurious lifestyle. In one of them, two such 'New Russians' are vying with each other. 'I bought this tie for a thousand US dollars,' says the first. 'You screwed up there!' says the other. 'There's a place round the corner where you can buy it at twice the price!'

Many of these people seemed to have come from nowhere, having no publicly known history. Many more had conspicuous criminal backgrounds. But the significant portion of wealth happened to belong not to these newcomers but to the elite emerging out of the old Soviet bureaucracy known as *nomenklatura*.

In fact, Russian privatization was no more than a redistribution of assets between different bureaucratic groups present in the Soviet system long before the new reforms began. The strategy of the liberal reforms of the 1990s was to give away national property for next to nothing and to break up the economic potential of the former superpower. It is a fact worth remembering that the Soviet Union

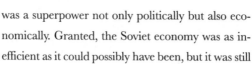

was a superpower not only politically but also economically. Granted, the Soviet economy was as inefficient as it could possibly have been, but it was still the second largest in the world.

Just before the start of the market reform, some economists calculated that there was not enough capital in Russia to buy out state-owned assets. The financial resources of the population were barely enough to cover 1 per cent of the assets about to be privatized. Of course, this depends on how much value you attribute to these assets. Anatoly Chubais, later known as 'the father of Russian privatization' (and now heading a public company set up to invest in the development of nanotechnologies), kept telling everybody that no adequate calculation of prices was possible because there was no market, and only the market can tell the real value of assets. Whether or not there was simply 'no market' in the USSR is open to debate, but the world market clearly existed and could give the reformers a clue to how much these assets may cost. Moreover, even if one had no idea about how much to pay for the factories being privatized, one could at least have an idea about the price of commodities. If the factory was sold for a price that was less than 5 per cent of the price of the products stockpiled in its warehouses, that tells us something. Very often, after privatization, the new owners sold the stored products and closed the factories. This procedure left them with profits of 500–1,000 per cent. Even selling the plant of privatized factories for scrap metal allowed these new entrepreneurs to make enormous fortunes.

In practice, most Soviet enterprises were privatized for less than 1 per cent of their market price— the economists of the late 1980s were overoptimistic. When, in 1993, after a *coup d'état*, the parliament building was taken over by the government, it was decided to protect it by putting up a fence. The cost of erecting this fence was far greater than the revenues raised for the State budget through privatizing most of its property. Only three Russian companies were sold for a sum that exceeded the cost of the fence.

Ironically, no matter how absurd, this process had its own logic. If you can't sell (because no one is going to buy), then you may as well give your property away. Foreign companies, of course, were ready to pay more money than the new Russian would-be proprietors, but they too were reluctant to pay too much: they had their eyes on the cream that the Russian elite intended to skim for itself. So, when raising money for the budget was out of question, the only real motivation for the process was to give away assets to friends, partners and allies.

It was the people who were already in power in the USSR during the late years of 'Communist' rule who formed the core of the new capitalist elite. Two-thirds of the capitalist class as it emerged in the 1990s had a party background. Some came from the old Soviet secret police, the KGB. Of course, some new arrivals were inevitable. Some of the new owners were at first no more than trustees who got a chance to manage money and assets for the party bosses and State functionaries who were unable for one or another reason to do it openly. Naturally, these trustees did not forget themselves; they often embezzled resources to build up their own fortunes. That was the story of many famous oligarchs. By the mid-1990s, the whole world had learned the names of Vladimir Gusinsky, Boris Berezovsky, Mikhail Khodorkovsky, Roman Abramovich and many others. But once the political and social situation in Russia began to stabilize, the newcomers began to lose their influence. And those of them who did not understand that their time had gone lost not only political and business influence but also much of their property.

Later, Western experts made loud lamentations about Russian corruption. Strangely enough, they did so *ex post facto*, when the process was complete and new property relations established. When in the early 1990s news of corruption and plunder in Russia began to reach Western observers, journalists and experts, many of whom were based in Moscow, they rejected it out of hand as 'Communist propaganda'. But, of course, they were familiar with these stories. Later, in the late 1990s, they readily quoted the very

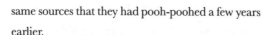

same sources that they had pooh-poohed a few years earlier.

However, corruption played a necessary regulatory role: it provided the only viable criteria for decision-making in the current circumstances. In other words, either you don't go for privatization at all, or you don't complain when it proves to be corrupt, pretty well undistinguishable from looting and plunder.

The privatization process was inevitably followed by a massive decline in production. Debate continues as to how much of GDP and industrial capacity was actually lost. Given the way that Russian statistics operated, one cannot expect all figures to be totally reliable, but even the most conservative account yields a figure of about 40 per cent loss in production and about 50 per cent decline in living standards. Some factories were closed because they could not compete in the liberalized market. Some were mismanaged and wrecked by their new owners. Finally, many enterprises suffered because of the disintegration of the USSR. Their suppliers and customers were located in different republics, which now became independent states with different currencies and economic rules and different regimes of privatization. They suffered when their partner companies closed down, changed their production plans or switched to other markets. Commodities formerly traded in the same currency were now to be traded in various different ones or bought for US dollars—the declining value of the Russian rouble itself caused quite a few bankruptcies.

ECONOMY IN DECAY

Out of the many enterprises owned by the Soviet Union, only the extracting industries managed to do reasonably well. Ironically, they even benefited from the decline of the other productive sectors. With industry collapsing, domestic demand for oil, gas and metals inevitably diminished, which left the extracting companies with more resources to be sold for hard currency in the world market.

Predictably, this decline in production was followed by social collapse. By 1992, the social crisis was so dramatic that even parliament, which earlier had given the green light to most reforms, was forced to react. Deputies had to respond to the pressure of their voters and started criticizing President Boris Yeltsin and his team of 'young reformers'. In fact, this criticism was quite modest and did not go beyond the conclusions that, in retrospect, were shared by most experts, including many pro-market ones. Moreover, parliament called for the reforms not to be abandoned, but, rather, 'corrected'. Many industrial managers sided with parliament in its attempt to save what was left of the former Soviet productive base.

The reaction of Yeltsin and his team of resolute reformers was fast and simple. All his critics were accused of being involved in Communist and fascist conspiracies. In 1993, parliament was dissolved and the Constitution suspended. This *coup d'état* was applauded by the leaders of all leading Western democracies, who also supported the violent measures used in Moscow to suppress the resistance that continued for two weeks.

The parliament, shelled by the tanks and burned, became a symbol of the new authoritarian State established in 1993. Western commentators noticed an authoritarian evolution of Russia only 10 years later, when Yeltsin's successor Vladimir Putin used his powers to weaken the positions of some oligarchs and criticized American policy in Iraq. However Putin, unlike Yeltsin, did not organize a *coup d'état*; he merely used the extraordinary powers bestowed on the president and his administration by Yeltsin's Constitution. He also brutally suppressed the rebellion in Chechnya, which had started under his predecessor. It was Yeltsin who bombed the Chechen capital, Grozny, back into the Middle Ages. The difference between the two presidents was not that one was more brutal than the other, but that the second used violence more effectively than the first.

The crisis of 1993 had some other consequences that were less visible and less debated, but no less important. Yeltsin's team had learned the lesson and did correct some aspects of the reform.

First, after repressing the political opposition, they made a deal with the managerial elite in industry, giving it ready access to the privatization process. Some of the productive assets were saved from destruction and later became the basis of Russia's industrial recovery. Finally, the government started re-creating some safety nets for the people who were suffering from its policies. All sorts of different categories of citizens started getting public benefits. They included old people, starving because of miserable pensions; teachers who tried to survive on starvation wages; workers suffering all sorts of diseases after struggling to contain the nuclear disaster in Chernobyl in 1986; and military officers who had no motivation to keep on serving their country because of low salaries and demoralization. All these categories of people were now entitled to various subsidies and benefits, such as riding buses for free or paying minimal rents for their flats.

By the end of the 1990s it seemed that the worst was over. Yeltsin was re-elected as president, surviving a challenge from Gennady Zyuganov, a nationalist politician posing as a Communist. Many say that there was electoral fraud, but, as long as the other side accepted its defeat and did not claim irregularities in the poll-count, it is safe to assume that it was a real victory.

The rouble seemed to be stable and a new middle class was emerging in Moscow and the major cities. Consumerist culture was gradually establishing itself, making people accept a new set of values and incentives. Eighty per cent of the population remained poor, but there was 20 per cent that felt quite satisfied with the way things were. Not too many in democratic terms, but enough for an authoritarian government to guarantee stability.

The only problem, which Yeltsin's team seemed unable to resolve, was how to relaunch Russia's industry. Economic growth was expected to resume in 1996, but it did not. Nor did it in 1997 or 1998.

One reason for this was the financial policy of the government, which was praised by global institutions such as the World Bank and the International Monetary Fund, as well as by many representatives of the home-grown middle class which was able to enjoy easy access to cheap imports. In other words, the Russian rouble was massively overvalued.

To keep inflation down and the exchange rate stable, the government cut its costs and tried to print as little money as possible. Comrade Stalin used to say: 'When there is a man, there is a problem. When there is no man, there is no problem.' Russian liberal economists followed the same logic. When there is money, there is inflation. No money, no inflation. This reluctance to print money led to a situation in which workers in both the private and the public sector failed to get their salaries paid for months on end. At the same time, the government lost taxation revenue from the impoverished population and declining industry and was forced to borrow. Its debt was growing daily. And, on top of all this, a global financial crisis was erupting after the crash of the

Thai baht in 1997. International oil prices were also declining, leaving Moscow no room for manoeuvre.

In August 1998, the Russian government defaulted on its domestic debt, and this was immediately followed by a currency crash. In September, *Moscow Times* claimed that the Russian rouble was the world's fastest-falling currency—quite an assertion, given the gloomy state of world finance at that time. On 16 August, the rouble stood at 6 against the dollar, in early September at 12. Next year, the exchange rate stabilized at 30.

Many banks crashed along with the currency. Even top civil servants had problems in drawing their salaries because credit cards were blocked by failing banks. The Kremlin was panicking and business leaders were demoralized. But this was the take-off point for the new Russia's economic expansion.

When imports collapsed, domestic producers started to recover. The cheap rouble made struggling companies competitive both at home and abroad. Jobs were created. And the government of a new

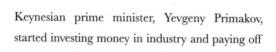

Keynesian prime minister, Yevgeny Primakov, started investing money in industry and paying off wage arrears.

Primakov's government was printing money and inflation was diminishing! This unique situation became possible only because the prices prior to the default were too high. Now, when money came back into the economy, prices began to get closer to the real demand.

Soon after the start of its industrial recovery, Russia got more good news. Global oil prices started rising. During the crisis period the price of oil was about US $17–18 per barrel. It almost doubled by the early 2000s and kept rising steadily throughout the following decade, reaching a record US $147–148 per barrel in 2008.

RUSSIAN REVIVAL

With their income rising, different layers of the Russian population could now enjoy the pleasures of consumerism that they could only dream of in Soviet times. And, along with the economy, cultural output was also reviving. Mexican soap operas were replaced by locally produced ones (though sometimes based on imported scenarios); cinemas showed not only movies made in Hollywood but quite a lot of titles from our native filmmakers. In fact, many of these products were Russian only nominally: more often than not, in cultural terms, these were American movies made by Russians. The old tradition of Soviet cinema was lost and something new had yet to be created. The publishing industry, moribund in the 1990s, was also doing well. A great many foreign books were translated, including encyclopaedias and history textbooks. Russian history became the subject of publications ranging from very serious research books to strange pamphlets trying to prove that Ancient Rome was an invention of Western conspirators who wanted to discredit Moscow as the one and only source of global civilization. All sorts of books were selling. For example, in the biggest Moscow bookshop, Dom Knigi, a survivor of the Soviet era, you could see a shelf labelled 'Jews', on which books dealing with the horrors of the Holocaust stood side by side with publications attacking Hitler for being too soft on the Jews.

The intellectual climate changed dramatically. In the early 1990s, Russians were hungry for anything Western, especially American. That forbidden fruit was now suddenly available. A decade later, the situation had changed. The debate between nationalists and Westernizers, more than a century old, was still raging, and this time pro-Western liberals were clearly lacking support not only among the general population but also inside the intellectual community. Nationalism was increasingly becoming endorsed by official circles as a new State ideology to fill the void left by the demise of Soviet Communism. However, the authorities took great care not to encourage the most extreme forms of Russian nationalism, which may provoke confrontation between different ethnic groups and destabilize the country. In this context, leftist ideas were visibly making inroads but this new intellectual turn was not yet being expressed in new political organizations or movements.

Though most people remained quite poor, in the streets of Moscow or St Petersburg you could now perhaps see more elegantly dressed people than in any other European capital. Car sales were rising so fast that all major international brands started their own factories in Russia to satisfy growing domestic demand, which was generated not only by the rich but also by the increasingly visible middle class.

The shower of petrodollars transformed Russian business, making it go global. I remember, in 2006, one of my friends returning from Africa. He was not in that part of the continent where tourists spend big money to take refuge in five-star resorts and the exotic tropics, but in an area which had long had no experience of welcoming a white person. And it wasn't the thirst for adventure that beckoned him there: a group of Russian businessmen had decided to start mining operations somewhere in the Congo.

Actually, they did have plenty of adventures. Two of the Russians came close to being killed: one for not speaking French, the other mistaken for a Ugandan spy. Each time they managed to save their own and their colleagues' lives fairly cheap—US $20.

When they stopped for a night in the only 'decent' hotel in a provincial town, a rat attacked them. They went down to reception to complain. 'And what room are you in?' asked an elderly black man, sitting at the desk. 'In 216? That rat's been living there for three months.'

The only thing left was to feed the rodent. The rat chilled out, moved to the bathroom and never bothered them again.

There was a lot more that the traveller shared with me, but, as I listened to his story, I suddenly realized that my friend was carrying out a mission of globalizing Russian capitalism, providing ways to export Russian capital. Missions like this one are not always dramatic. Usually the adventures come to small and medium-sized businesses. Large corporations do not have such problems. If they do, they make others foot the bill.

By 2006, Gazprom's capitalization positioned it third on the world list. Having so vast a share of the country's energy resources under their control, Russian companies initially looked all set to reach the top of the world rankings. It did not happen then, because all these enterprises in the course of privatization were dramatically underestimated.

Of course, capital outflow is typical not only of core capitalist countries like the US, the EU nations or Japan and South Korea; Brazil, South Africa, Turkey and India are all setting up transnational companies of their own and China has followed suit. However, the coming of Russia's own transnational corporations does indicate the maturity of our capitalism. Gone are the fun times when a Russian nouveau riche, fresh off the plane at Heathrow airport, would make a beeline for the nearest broker, trying to unload stolen money into some offshore fund. Now it's not just money being syphoned away, but capital deliberately invested, for strategic purposes. Gazprom systematically buys out companies in the countries of the former Eastern Bloc, then moves on to the West, taking over transportation and distribution networks for its products. Norilsk Nickel and Lukoil acquire enterprises abroad which could either become their partners or competitors. Automobile manufacturers, having bought a motor plant, debate whether they should move it to Russia or let it stay where it is, just making it a part of their processing chain.

Of course, this new transnational status creates new problems for the Russian corporations involved. It brings new concerns about the company's image, a need to consider public opinion, not so much back home as abroad. This issue remains very poorly resolved with us. Sometimes, while business leaders are preoccupied with building a favourable image with foreigners, things at home are getting worse.

Russia's oil wealth gives our companies prospects for global expansion. The trouble is that, inside Russia, roads are still impassable, buildings collapse on their occupants' heads, and the equipment in most plants and factories would make fine exhibits in a museum of twentieth-century technology. Nothing is going to change the situation, as investments of this kind are not attractive in modern terms. Having become global players, Russian companies tend to use all of their competitive advantages in the world market, partly through lack of time or concern for their own country, but primarily because it is not profitable to invest in development at home.

Western countries became advanced within the capitalist world because they entered the global market having already been leaders in their field—in the majority of fields—ranging from technologies through transport infrastructure, even to ideology. For them, globalization has been a way to support and expand their leadership. For countries on the periphery, such success may turn into disaster. An American capitalist might say: 'What is good for General Motors is good for America.' Before accepting that, go ahead and ask members of the trade unions at his plants what they think, and the results will not be that optimistic. But if you are told: 'What is good for Gazprom is good for Russia,' then no one will even need additional asking.

BUREAUCRATS VS OLIGARCHS

In the 2000s, Russia's new economic stability was guaranteed by the power of a bureaucracy that both controlled the population politically and was trying to discipline the oligarchy in the economic sphere. The excesses of the 1990s, when the irresponsible behaviour of business leaders became self-evident, had to be stopped. The elites had to accept that the state was both providing security and demanding responsibility. This combination was at the heart of the new stability, promised and delivered by the Russian government, after Putin inherited the post of president from the ageing and sick Yeltsin.

The bureaucracy itself was more and more involved in business. Civil servants often took key

positions in huge mixed corporations that were neither private nor public, like the notorious *parastatales*
of Latin America, becoming their shareholders and
using their State power to serve the special interests
of these companies. In this respect, the relations
between the State and the former oligarchic structures are reversed but not greatly changed. Putin's
team was deeply involved with the Gazprom corpo-
ration, which in many cases could dictate its policies
to the Kremlin (for example, price increases for fuel
undermined Russia's position in the former Soviet
zone, including not only pro-Western Ukraine but
also a pro-Russian Belarus).

In principle, these conditions were good for
everyone. While the bureaucracy could rule, the oligarchs were left to make their money. In general, the
culture of business was changing from an oligarchic
to a corporate one. This was the new stage of capitalism, which was not about loot any more but about
organizing production and making profits from it.
Alas, not everybody seemed happy with this
arrangement. Some of the most prominent oligarchs

of the 1990s were used to wielding not just economic but also political power, directly controlling the government, appointing or sacking ministers or provincial governors, sometimes even acting as kingmakers, trying to control the presidency itself. The rules of the game under Yeltsin, but not any more under Putin. Not only the rules, but the game itself now changed. And while the lesser oligarchs were quite happy to become Western-style CEOs, the foremost among them kept on contending for direct political control.

Throughout the early 2000s the conflict between the different clans has intensified. On the one hand there are the so-called St Petersburg 'Chekists' (former officers of the Soviet secret police, known as the Cheka long before it became famous as the KGB), who swept to power on President Putin's coat-tails, although not all of them are members of the State security establishment. Then there is the oligarch old guard—those who climbed the greasy pole under Yeltsin and acquired the Family clout— though far from all of them are intimately related to the former president's family. The standoff between these groups was all too real. And there was plenty to fight over: at stake was power and control of the country's assets.

The first group of 'oligarchs' to come to blows with the Putin administration was the same group which, in 1999, had played a central role in making him President of Russia. Because of their role in these events, they expected to be able to control the administration. They miscalculated. In 2001–03, one by one, the powerful oligarchs of the Yeltsin Family started losing ground. Boris Berezovsky and Vladimir Gusinsky had to leave the country, after losing most of their property there. Roman Abramovich, who seemed to be the third most influential member of this group, made a deal with the Kremlin and was allowed not only to continue as the Governor of Chukotka in the Far East but also to share the spoils of Berezovsky's demise. Assets of the Sibneft Oil Company that earlier belonged to Berezovsky somehow ended up in Abramovich's hands. When the government started putting pressure on him, Abramovich did not retaliate. He merely found a much safer investment in buying a Chelsea soccer club in England.

However, the most dramatic confrontation involved Mikhail Khodorkovsky's Yukos group. After the demise of the Family, he clearly tried to take over the place left vacant by Berezovsky. Yukos was not just one of the biggest Russian oil companies (along with Lukoil, Sibneft and TNK) but also a major player in our political and cultural life. It was one of those dozen or so companies that control most of the economy. These very same corporations and people also control most of the big media. (What is not under their control is in the hands of the government.) And they sponsor cultural events, sporting teams, scientific and educational projects. Needless to say, these same people influence politics. This is exactly what the ancient Greeks called 'oligarchy': rule by a few.

Of all the oligarchs, Khodorkovsky was the most prominent and definitely the most intelligent, so an attack on him was highly symbolic. Both the Chekists and the Family know that the main threat they face is from each other—and they have taken out insurance accordingly.

In July 2003, with the arrest of Platon Lebedev, the conflict between certain sectors of the oligarchy and the Kremlin led to a new outbreak of hostilities. Lebedev was a leading executive of the powerful Menatep Group and a major shareholder in Yukos. Not only was Lebedev arrested, but the Yukos CEO, Khodorkovsky, and his right-hand man, Leonid Nevzlin, were called into the Prosecutor General's office for questioning. Over the weekend, Khodorkovsky commented on these events as follows: 'This concerns neither the company's management nor its business activities. This concerns individual company shareholders.' He hit the nail on the head. It is the interests of 'individual people' that lie at the heart of the Russian political system—and the names of most of these individuals are no big secret.

Pro-Kremlin court experts explained to the masses that Putin had finally decided to take on the oligarchs. The vast majority of the population, who had suffered impoverishment during the course of the 1990s, were likely to be well-disposed towards such moves. In the oligarchs they see if not those who are to blame for their woes then at least those who got very rich off the situation.

Soon, Nevzlin had to flee to Israel and Khodorkovsky was arrested. Since then, his supporters have declared him a political prisoner. His enemies call him a delinquent and a thief. I can agree with both sides. I suppose he can be called a political prisoner, but not a prisoner of conscience. Prisoners of conscience are people who are jailed by a regime because of their principles and ideas, which conflict with those of the authorities. This does not apply to Khodorkovsky. He found himself in prison precisely because he shared the principles basic to the current order.

The first of these is the credo that power and money should be indivisible, that the ruling clique should consist of the wealthy elite, controlling the gullible masses through the media and corrupt parliamentarians. This view of politics is shared by both sides in the Russian power struggle. Both the government and its adversaries have done their best to preserve the results of privatization. Both have aimed to concentrate power in their hands by elbowing their opponents aside and not thinking too hard about any moral implications.

It was exactly because the directors of Yukos did not differ from the tenants of the Kremlin that the ruling clique considered them to be really dangerous. And therefore took stringent measures. Khodorkovsky is a political prisoner only in the mediaeval sense, as when great lords and princes were jailed in the Bastille or the Tower of London after failed plots.

The problem does not reside in whether Khodorkovsky's sentence is correct from a legal point of view, but in the fact that the Russian authorities tried to formalize within the categories of contemporary law a conflict that does not, by definition, fit into democratic political standards. When a struggle with no rules at all is underway, it is meaningless to appeal to due process after the event. What we see here is not a battle of principles and ideas, but a struggle for power in the most cynical and transparent form. It is impossible to reach a righteous decision in a situation with no right sides at all. And the degree of legality of a winner's or loser's position is deeply indifferent for us, the serfs of the Russian State.

Skirmishes with the oligarchs do not mean that the demise of the oligarchy is at hand. No structural reforms have been proposed by the Kremlin to restrict the economic power of the oligarchy, not even out of populist considerations. Nationalization was not on the agenda. Some Yukos assets finally ended up confiscated by the State, but, at the same time, the privatization of public property continued, and all major State corporations were turned into joint-stock companies that went public, selling their shares to private investors both at home and abroad.

The St Petersburg Chekists, in moving against the Family, were not remotely interested in changing the system. On the contrary, they simply wanted to be the dominant players within it. They were seeking to use their political power to seize the 'commanding heights' of the economy. In the early 1990s, this was called 'converting power into property'. The dream of the St Petersburg Chekists, who missed the party the first time around, was to preside over a new carve-up. And in many ways they succeeded.

GUIDED DEMOCRACY

The current political situation in Russia can be characterized as fragile stability. Putin's administration was very much in control throughout his term in office. The war in Chechnya, which in the mid-1990s turned into a major disaster for the Yeltsin regime, came to some sort of successful end under Putin. It was not so much that the Russian military was able to suppress the guerrilla activities of the separatists as it was the Moscow politicians buying out the separatists' field commanders, who finally became the rulers of Chechnya but who paid the price of accepting Russian sovereignty. Provincial governors, who in the 1990s behaved like feudal lords, were also, more or less, brought to heel, naturally at the price of restricting formal democratic rights—they are not elected any more, but appointed by the president. Though this appointment must be confirmed by local assemblies, so far nobody has ever dared say 'No'.

Putin's next success was his ability to effectively eliminate political parties from public life without actually banning anyone. After 1993, the State Duma had so little power that parties whose role is limited to contesting elections to this body and to even less powerful local assemblies started losing ground in society, supposing that they ever enjoyed much public support. The main opposition force, the Communist Party of the Russian Federation (KPRF), is facing extinction (36 per cent in 1996, 24 per cent in 1999, 13 per cent in 2004 and 11.6 per cent in 2007). And the void cannot be filled: new legislation makes it technically impossible to establish a political party without the clear permission, or even support, of the administration.

Political freedoms are increasingly limited—not as much as is claimed in the liberal media, but nevertheless substantially. TV is totally controlled by the administration, and the main newspapers have been taken over by the State bureaucracy (usually through *parastatales*). Electoral legislation has been changed to prevent minor groups participating in the process, and electoral fraud remains a daily experience. The government-sponsored United Russia Party is expanding its presence in every aspect of public life (including 'sponsoring' textbooks for children in schools). Sometimes it is compared to the old Communist Party of the Soviet Union, but a more accurate comparison may be made with the Mexican Partido Revolucionario Institucional (PRI) in the 1970s and 1980s. United Russia is also paternalistic and includes different, sometimes conflicting, elements (from free-market liberals to paternalistic bureaucrats).

United Russia acts as both player and referee by setting or changing the rules as it chooses. Liberals have been outraged by this flagrant violation of democratic principles, but most people are openly indifferent—and rightly so. After all, what difference does it make for us if the rules of the political game are fair or unfair when the game itself bears no relationship to our lives and when we find the whole spectacle deeply offensive? In the end, the people are the main prize for the candidates. The election winners get to order us around, to rob us and deceive us.

The people are indifferent not so much to democracy as to a system that they cannot influence in any way. It is perfectly understandable that so many Russians have so little desire to follow election campaigns on television. They know by instinct that the politicians are fundamentally unable to speak the truth.

Perhaps the most important aspect of the new electoral law was the decision to eliminate the 'against all' option on the ballot paper. After all, this was nothing but a farce. The 'against all' concept was developed to convey the impression that voters had a legitimate way of expressing their protest at the ballot box. We should thank United Russia's deputies and the Central Elections Commission for removing this option from the ballot. Now we can stay at home and ignore the elections in peace.

In addition, politicians did the right thing when they removed the electoral rule that set a minimum threshold for voter turnout. The authorities understand that it is just not realistic to expect ordinary mortals to take part in the electoral process. Removing the burden of voter turnout, our leaders have shown their humanitarian credentials by not demanding anything from the people.

The cancellation of the minimum turnout means that the 2007 Duma elections were, technically speaking, more honest than the previous round. Back then, most ballot-box stuffing occurred at the local level where it was necessary to collect a minimum percentage of votes. If the threshold was not met, the elections had to be declared invalid according to the law, forcing people to repeat the whole performance. With the new rule in force, life has be-

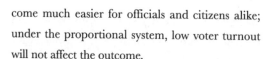
come much easier for officials and citizens alike; under the proportional system, low voter turnout will not affect the outcome.

It would be more honest to simply cancel elections altogether and let the politicians fight it out among themselves to determine who gets Duma seats. Even better would be to have them draw lots, or deputies may try to win seats by playing poker or throwing dice. Any of these methods would be fairer and more democratic than the present one. In addition, watching such a high-stakes contest would be far more entertaining. At least we could limit ourselves to being observers rather than participants in the spectacle. After all, when you go to the horse races, no one requires you to run after the horses.

To make parliamentary elections look more or less pluralistic, the Kremlin has established its own version of a two-party system. People have a choice between United Russia and the party headed by Federation Council Speaker Sergei Mironov, which opted for the name A Just Russia. Its politics and ideas do not differ much from those of United Russia, but this does not mean that there is no genuine competition between the two groups. Political and social considerations have little influence on the success of Russian parties. The real struggle takes place within the bureaucratic apparatus, and here the appearance of a second party changes a lot.

There is often a kind of pluralism within a bureaucratic apparatus—bureaucrats are prone to widespread dislikes and rivalries. But keeping up the appearance of unity within this hierarchy requires that all this chicanery remains behind closed doors. Orders from above have to be executed, and any open resistance is seen as breaching the basic principles of State service.

Bureaucrats can clandestinely sabotage orders, especially when everyone acknowledges how stupid an order is. But the image of unity has to be maintained with the dedication of a well-drilled guards unit on the parade ground.

But differences are part of life in political debate, even if there is little or no difference between rivals. Two candidates for the same office have to convince voters that they differ in more than just name.

Unfortunately, the public and bureaucratic spheres are so intertwined that they have apparently changed places. Politicians, regardless of party, understand clearly that they are really State servants who, for some reason, are formally elected. Bureaucrats, meanwhile, know that they make the serious political decisions.

Any spat between a department head and his deputy is much more important than a debate between faction leaders in the State Duma, let alone regional assemblies. But these skirmishes could take political shape at some point and kickstart a standoff at the ballot box.

THREATS TO STABILITY

Of course, the defeated oligarchs from the Family and Yukos clans have not sat idle, watching the triumph of Guided Democracy, Putin-style. They organize for a *revanche*, using as a model the 'colour revolutions' that happened in Georgia, Ukraine and the Kyrgyz Republic.

The Yukos Group, which has become the main sponsor of liberal opposition, continues to work with different political currents, trying to function as a kind of strategic centre for most of these projects. Because the liberals (the Union of Right-Wing Forces, the Yabloko Party and others) themselves lack public support, the concept of a United Opposition was propagated. According to this concept, liberals are supposed to cooperate with the KPRF. This party itself is very closely connected with different nationalist groups, including a neofascist umbrella organization, the Movement Against Illegal Immigration (DPNI). The name alone is telling, but let it not cause confusion: this group is not opposed merely to illegal immigrants; it objects to all ethnic minorities as well as to homosexuals. Another partner of the KPRF is the National Bolshevik Party of Eduard Limonov, a talented fascist writer and poet very popular with liberal glossy magazines. Yet another nationalist force, sometimes in competition with the KPRF, was the 'Rodina' Party, which developed its own vision of an Orange revolution based on 'Russian values'. In December 2005, Rodina was officially removed from electoral ballots for its racist propaganda and, later, altogether eliminated from politics by the administration, thus leaving the fascist movement without parliamentary representation—a fact that was publicly lamented by the liberal media.

The United Opposition has formed itself into two 'columns'. The first is more or less respectable and proposes a political agenda; the other plays the role of shock troops destabilizing the situation. The KPRF leadership aims to play an intermediate (and thus strategic) role, being involved with both.

A final point worth noting is that the struggle is not just between government and opposition but also within the government. Different sections of the administration are establishing connections with different currents of opposition, trying to manipulate them and use them for their own agendas. Those who lose out in the internal bureaucratic battles can be drawn towards supporting a destabilization scenario.

The problem with all these political combinations has been their total lack of mass support. An odd coalition of liberals, hard-line Communists and fascists did not attract much sympathy with the masses, especially because these opposition forces never worked out any social or economic programme other than the need to overthrow the 'criminal regime'.

This does not mean, however, that there has been no opposition from below. It comes in the form of semi-spontaneous social movements and free trade unions.

Trade union rights are severely restricted, and the biggest union formation is under government control—the Federation of Independent Trade Unions of Russia (FNPR). Most strikes since 2001 have been illegal. Nevertheless, independent labour unions are on the rise.

Because Russia is not yet a member of the World Trade Organization (WTO), a few sectors of the local economy continue to enjoy some State protection, most notably the automobile industry. This has led to an impressive amount of foreign direct investment: global companies have to assemble cars inside Russia in order to avoid paying high tariffs and to get their share of a growing local market. The same can be said about the production of refrigerators, microwave ovens and other domestic appliances. The growth of the manufacturing sector has been accompanied by a return of trade union militancy—the number of strikes rose visibly throughout 2005–06. This new militancy was also expressed in the growth of the second-biggest labour federation, the All-Russian Confederation of Labour (VKT), opposed to the State-controlled FNPR. The new VKT leadership elected in 2005 made its leftward political orientation very clear and opted for a strategy of 'aggressive organizing'.

Living standards have improved, and now come close on average to the level of late 1970, though with much higher social and regional differentiation. However, even after years of economic growth, many Russians are much poorer than in the late Soviet period. Social inequality is not getting any less dramatic—in fact, there is statistical evidence to show that it is still increasing. The positive average figures are produced by the growth of middle-class consumption in the big cities. These middle classes (including blue-collar workers in the oil and gas sectors as well as in the dominant international companies) consume most of the fruits of economic growth, leaving the workers who produce all this wealth far behind.

The economic success of capitalism has not led to the end of social struggles but, rather, has transformed them. Of course, the period that followed the default of 1998 was relatively calm. After the disasters and calamities of the 1990s, most people were emotionally drained. Then some improvement occurred, but that merely strengthened the general political apathy. With a government that seems to be reasonably competent and able to deliver the goods, why bother with politics?

However, this apathetic consent towards the current state of affairs could continue only as long as the ruling elite seemed to be abandoning the neoliberal policies of the 1990s. But, in January 2005, the Russian government announced a whole set of measures aimed at revoking the system of safety nets established during the previous decade. The rationale was simple: these safety nets contradicted the logic of the market and created obstacles to the commercialization and privatization of the social sphere. They had been necessary when massive impoverishment threatened the very survival of certain sectors of the population. Now that the economy was in somewhat better shape, there seemed to be no need for such structures. People should take care of themselves.

To smooth over the transition process, the government offered some compensation for the eliminated benefits ('monetization', in bureaucratese).

This compensation was inadequate and it involved humiliating paperwork, the joy of all bureaucracies. The streets exploded. All at once there were mass protests all over the country. Demonstrating in the middle of a Russian winter is not easy, and it is possible that the authorities had deliberately chosen January as the best time to launch unpopular measures. But the cold weather did not freeze popular discontent. Thousands of angry people (many of them retired men and women) blocked the streets, besieged government offices and fought with the police. And the police themselves were reluctant to disperse these crowds because they too had lost benefits.

About 2.5 million people were involved in the protest, and, though the government modified its policies in 2005, the main strategic trend did not change. In 2006, two more reforms were launched: housing reform hit hardest, increasing the costs paid by the public and leading to evictions of those unable to pay. So far the number of people evicted from their flats and houses has not been large, but it is rising and is becoming a very disturbing factor in social life. And the evictions made possible under the new legislation do not affect only those who cannot pay: this June, there was a real battle between police contingents and some inhabitants of Butovo (a suburb of Moscow) whose houses were going to be demolished.

Educational reform has followed the same free-market principles. Labour laws keep changing for the worse. Environmental policies are a disaster, including a free-market Water Code and an ultra-liberal Forest Code (this last one is still in preparation).

No surprise then that all these government policies have created a groundswell for mass resistance, expressed through strikes, demonstrations and riots that happen almost daily. But, unlike the spectacular movement of January 2005, these protests are usually limited to local issues and do not get reported by the mass media, especially abroad. Some events draw national attention, such as the railway strike in Moscow in 2008 when the traffic between the province and the capital city was paralysed. Many more go unreported.

If the month of November 2007 is remembered, it will not be for the election campaign, or the Kremlin's political intrigues, but for the upsurge in worker protests. Prominent among these was the strike at the Ford factory in Vsevolozhsk, near St Petersburg, the first open-ended strike in Russia since President Putin came to office in 2000. In a sense it sums up this epoch.

This longest and most intense standoff in post-Soviet times began on 20 November and continued for three weeks, till 14 December. According to union activists, the plant's assembly line came to a total stop. Then management, by hook or by crook, recruited first a shift of office workers, and, towards the end of the strike, a second shift, to keep the line running. But the quality control department continued its strike, which means that cars produced in early December may not meet all of their technical standards.

During the strike, only a small number of cars came off the assembly line, and the company can expect to be counting its losses for a long time to come. And the striking workers, for their part, are now morally and physically exhausted after fighting a long battle against management. The labour union's strike fund was unprepared for such a protracted battle, OMON special-purpose militia units harassed the picketers and the strike's organizers were threatened with prosecution.

In the end, a general meeting of striking Ford workers voted in a secret ballot to halt the protest, and the company's administration promised to raise their wages. Both sides signed an agreement prohibiting punitive actions against the strike's participants. The union and the company promised to settle all matters of dispute by 1 February. Union leader Alexei Etmanov said the Ford administration was prepared to index salaries to keep pace with inflation and to provide additional pay for extra work and for long service in the company. Etmanov characterized all of this as a victory, saying: 'This strike turned out to be the most protracted in the last 10 years. I think the administration should agree to concessions. They would hardly want to see a new strike in the spring.'

The union achieved much less than expected, however. In addition to the concessions obtained, workers had demanded a 30 per cent wage increase, higher pensions and changes in the work schedule and the number of hours worked per day.

It would seem that the confrontation ended in a draw. The management failed to break the union, and the striking workers walked away with only modest gains, especially considering the tremendous effort and stress they endured to get what they wanted.

The conflict at the Ford factory assumed a significance far beyond the organization itself and even beyond the auto-manufacturing industry in Russia. Media from all over the country covered the story extensively. This was the first open-ended strike since the new Labour Code came into force several years before. It was also the first strike that the authorities did not crush and in which its participants obtained a guarantee that they would not be subjected to reprisals. The strike showed once again that Russia's laws work against the labour unions, but it also showed that strong workers' organizations can find ways to get around many of those restrictions.

Finally, the Ford conflict forced many people to acknowledge that factory workers are shamefully underpaid in Russia—not only as compared with Western Europe but also with respect to similar car plants in Latin American countries.

Ultimately, the fundamental issues in this strike concern not only Ford workers and managers but all of society. Although the Ford factory is working again, and things seem to be back to normal, we must all draw these important conclusions from this strike and understand that serious labour problems persist in the country. The first stone has been thrown into the water, and the ripples will travel for a very long time.

Our labour laws are absurd. They are ostensibly designed to allow labour strikes but, in reality they make them illegal. But the labour unions often find ways around the legal limitations. For example they can stage a walkout for one day, and, after receiving a court injunction that prohibits strike activity, they will obey the law by cancelling the strike. Some time later, this pattern is repeated—one day, they strike; next day, they call it off.

At the Ford factory, however, workers rejected this cat-and-mouse game and upped the stakes by declaring an open-ended strike even though rank-and-file union members and their leaders knew full well that there could be serious reprisals. The people of St Petersburg are well aware of what happened to the leaders of the city's postal workers' union. Not long after their strike began, the organizer, Maxim Roshchin, was dismissed. The deputy head of the union, Dmitry Patsuk, was also fired soon after. Contesting his wrongful dismissal in court, Patsuk continues to negotiate with the administration, but now as a representative of the VKT, an umbrella organization that includes the St Petersburg postal workers' union. This is not the only case when punitive measures have been brought against workers demanding their rights. Valery Sokolov, leader of the labour union at Heineken's brewery in St Petersburg, was dismissed following a work slowdown staged there in April. Before that, Sergei Dolgy, chairman of the first Coca-Cola employees' union, was fired in similar fashion.

These repressive measures, however, have failed to quell labour unrest. At the height of the Ford factory strike, workers learned that two members of the union, who were fired last summer for striking at the AvtoVAZ factory in Tolyatti, had been reinstated following negotiations between the factory administration and the VKT. Ford workers had supported their Tolyatti colleagues during the summer strike. Now Tolyatti workers were expressing solidarity by sending money to the Ford workers' union.

This solidarity sometimes assumes unusual forms. A group of young artists and philosophers who publish the newspaper *What Is to Be Done?* sent an open letter to the strikers at Vsevolozhsk expressing their gratitude for the fact that the workers' actions provided them with creative inspiration. Corporations are gradually getting used to the idea that Russian workers also have rights, and that it is necessary to take union demands into account. The punitive measures that businesses enacted last summer have been largely ineffective. A victory for one union serves as an example for others. The tide is rising.

In late November 2007, train engineers planned a strike, but they were compelled to call it off after receiving a court injunction and threats of reprisals from the authorities. A few months later they finally went on strike, knowing that their action would be considered illegal. In effect, workers are forced to break the law in order to demand their rights, but this is the only option available for unions to achieve justice. This is a true democratic struggle that people understand much better than the abstract slogans offered by the liberal opposition. To the government's relief, there is almost no way that these protests will ever join hands with the activities of the opposition, whose leaders criticize the Kremlin for too little free market, too little neoliberalism.

A MURDER FOR EXPORT

By the end of Putin's term, Russia's reputation in the West was going from bad to worse. The liberal opposition, failing to attract public sympathy at home, addressed the Western media, where it got much more attention and understanding. On the other hand, sections of Russia's own security apparatus were glad of the growing tension, because, for them, confrontation meant new investment, promotions and political influence.

When a famous journalist, Anna Politkovskaya, was murdered in Moscow, Putin was immediately accused by the opposition of being behind the crime. The president seemed furious. What did he have to gain from taking out a contract on a journalist? Politkovskaya was a harsh critic of the Chechen war, but, since the decline of the war, she had been less and less active. It made no sense for Putin to kill her, but it made a lot of sense for other players.

When Politkovskaya was killed, I predicted that there would be a sequel to this story. Unfortunately, I was right. Alexander Litvinenko died in London, and this made headlines, but in Britain rather than in Russia. Which is perfectly logical—the English people would not just stand by and watch a political exile granted British asylum being murdered.

A few days after the event, Scotland Yard confirmed publicly that Litvinenko, a former KGB officer admitted to British citizenship only a month ago, had been poisoned. Along with this announcement, just as one would have expected, Litvinenko's employer, or at least his sponsor in London, Boris Berezovsky, hastened to name the main suspect—Vladimir Putin.

In a further twist to the plot, the assault on Litvinenko seemed to be connected to the assassination of Politkovskaya. The investigators believed that the former KGB agent was poisoned in a Japanese restaurant where he met with an Italian journalist who allegedly possessed data concerning the Politkovskaya case. After being interrogated by

British detectives, the journalist, fearful for his life, went to ground somewhere in Italy.

Litvinenko had accused the Kremlin and the Russian intelligence agencies of paving Putin's way to power by staging a series of explosions in apartment blocks in Moscow and elsewhere back in 1999, with considerable loss of life. These blasts really did help the regime, by rallying public opinion behind it. Some of Litvinenko's arguments were quite convincing, some were weak. In any case, the affair of the apartment block explosions will never be solved, just as the true story of the 11 September terrorist attack in the US or the murder of John F. Kennedy and many other high-profile cases of the twentieth century will never be revealed. History has plenty of similar examples, such as the disappearance of the princes in the Tower of London in the mid-fifteenth century. The case was never solved, or even properly investigated. It is a cold case to this day.

As a rule, the official version loses its credibility in the course of time, while alternative versions lack evidence and the authorities blatantly refuse to ex-

amine and thus to deflate them. Private investiga-
tions generate contradictory facts and speculations.
But the verdict is delivered by public opinion, which
is always set against the powers that be.

Under the prevailing circumstances, to stir up
the ghosts of the past would have been highly dis-
advantageous tactics for the Russian administration.
Litivinenko, residing in London, was not a thorn in
the side of the Russian authorities, in particular because his version of the Moscow explosions was only
one among many, and not the most convincing. But
take out the former KGB agent in a sensational assassination and his accusations gain credibility: the
whole affair moves to the front burner. The Kremlin's foes jumped at the chance to use the poisoning
of Litvinenko as one more argument against the authorities, and to link it to such cases as the shooting
of Politkovskaya and the apartment block explosions
in 1999. Moscow was again seen from the West as
the capital of an 'evil Empire'.

It is only at first sight that the prominent critics
of the present regime look like the only victims of

these events. If we delve deeper, we find that the authorities are extremely vulnerable to such developments. The fatal blows hit only the commentators on the Great Game, leaving opposition leaders safe and sound. As a result the opposition gets its martyrs and the authorities come under suspicion. In these circumstances, pro-Kremlin analysts have every reason for claiming that Litvinenko's poisoning and Politovskaya's murder were pure provocations, and that it was the opposition itself, and Berezovsky in person, who organized it all in order to discredit the Kremlin's ruling elite.

For all that, it is difficult to think of Berezovsky trying to kill his closest associate in London. However vicious he may be, he is not crazy. Berezovsky would be bound to understand that, once Scotland Yard found a link, he would not get away with it.

The 1999 explosions in Moscow, Buynaksk and Volgodonsk reflected the struggle for power within the ruling elite. The murders of Politkovskaya and Litvinenko revealed that, behind Putin's consolidation of the elite, that struggle continued. Neither

President Putin nor Berezovsky would contract such murders—for both, the backlash outweighs any possible gain.

However, if we look at these events from the point of view of a succession struggle in the Kremlin, the picture changes. Undermining Russia's position in the world would permit the political elites to retain control over the new president coming to power in the Kremlin at the end of Putin's term. The name of the new leader had not yet been announced, but the struggle around his office had already begun.

THE NEW PRESIDENT

Putin presided over economic growth and recovery. Though, of course, his administration took maximum political advantage of this situation, it was an easy task. But, in 2008, his term in office was due to end.

The transfer of power to the next president became the key topic in Russian politics. Who would take over after Putin, and how would the succession be managed? The struggle for nomination began between a more liberal trend in the administration, backed by the finance and economic ministries, and the *siloviki*, representing the security apparatus. These bureaucratic groups were the only real players on the political field, because liberal opposition was decaying and the Left remained powerless and sectarian. United Russia remained the dominant political force in 2007 and 2008, but it lacked a clear perspective. Without the support of the senior bureaucracy, it was nothing.

After some months of confusion, we witnessed a strange kind of 'primary' that only Russia could have concocted. Two unofficial candidates came forward. Watching Deputy Prime Minister Dmitry Medvedev and the other first deputy prime minister, Sergei Ivanov, vie for the chance to become Putin's successor was no less entertaining than the Democratic primary contest between Barack Obama and Hillary Clinton in America. The only difference is that the US primaries invite the media and ordinary citizens to take part in the process, while the Russian primaries take place behind closed doors, in the offices of Moscow's political elite.

The result of these differences is that, while US presidential candidates make campaign pledges long before the election and then don't keep them once inside the White House, a Russian candidate conceals his agenda from the public and reveals it only after becoming president. I don't know which system is better, but I am firmly convinced that ours is more interesting. It encourages conjecture and gives us countless opportunities for guessing at future events. It is true, however, that these predictions are invariably followed by surprises, usually unpleasant.

People were constantly guessing and waiting. First, we tried to guess the name of the next president, and then, when Medvedev's name was announced and formal elections held, we speculated as to what his agenda might be. Political analysts and journalists tried to figure out what Medvedev's future programme would look like, based on a few casual remarks and gestures. The future leader fed our imaginations with vague references to possible political changes. A clue to Medvedev's future, however, could be found by looking at the stock market indexes, the price of oil and the consumer price index. Today, while analysts attempt to read between the lines of Medvedev's elliptical remarks, government officials still can't for the life of them figure out the cause of the country's persistently high inflation. The whole difference between Putin's eight years in office and what we will see under President Medvedev can be summed up as follows: Putin ruled during a bull market, and Medvedev was left trying to deal with a bearish economy.

Economic growth didn't lead to resolving any structural problems. Most of Russia's industrial plant and infrastructure is ageing and very little public investment is taking place. The economy continues to be dependent on oil and gas sales, technological research is declining, dependence on the international market is increasing.

After 1999, we saw stable economic growth based mainly on high oil prices. Of course, when the oil prices fall, the economy will follow. Still, there are other causes of economic growth which have to be mentioned: the rouble crash in 1998 led to a massive devaluation of local currency and much of the domestic market was regained by domestic producers.

The stability under Putin was based on the fact that the country's elites were able to compromise when necessary, yet still get everything they wanted. Yukos was a good example. Russia's largest oil company was torn to pieces, but the elite divvied up the spoils among themselves and enjoyed the huge feast together in peace.

A global economic crisis could change this peaceful coexistence among the feuding Kremlin clans. Competing groups would attempt to undermine each other through polemics and sharp accusations, and this, paradoxically, would resemble an active, pluralistic debate on political issues.

Medvedev started his term with vague liberal promises, clearly thinking of a rapprochement with

the West, in the context of worsening Russian–
American relations. Though it was clearly not Russia's fault that the international situation was
worsening. No matter how eager the Kremlin was
to compromise with Washington, the policies of
George W. Bush provoked one crisis after another.
Russia somehow accommodated to the eastwards
expansion of the North Atlantic military alliance; it
protested against the occupation of Iraq, but swal-
lowed it. Yet every Russian concession was only followed by a new and even more aggressive initiative
by Washington and its client governments in the former Communist countries.

The final blow was the Georgian invasion of
the breakaway republic of South Ossetia. For more
than 10 years, Ossetian security had been guaranteed by Russia; and this fact was accepted interna-
tionally. It was more than clear that the Georgian
leadership wasn't going to change the rules unilat-
erally without having Washington's backing. And
this American backing was exactly the reason for
Georgia's President Mikhail Saakashvili to be sure

that Russia would simply sit back and do nothing. But enough is enough: Russian forces fought back. They moved into South Ossetia and then into Georgia itself, provoking a new international crisis.

This was clearly not Medvedev's original plan.

THE GEORGIAN WAR

Of course, in the West the conflict between Russia and Georgia was interpreted as evidence of Russia's neo-imperialist ambitions, and the role of the US in the Georgian offensive didn't merit great attention in the mainstream press. But the fundamental reasons behind this US–Russian confrontation differed profoundly from the Western media's version.

There have always been problems with the Georgian breakaway republics of South Ossetia and Abkhazia. And yes, there have been many points of contention between Moscow and Washington. But why has it all erupted into such a heightened confrontation right now? Most important, why have bilateral relations deteriorated so much, even when both sides are seeking compromises to limit the scale of the conflict?

In order to understand what is happening, we must take a step back from the situation in the Caucasus and even from current US–Russian relations. We are now witnessing the crisis in the global economic system.

In response to events in South Ossetia, the West threatened to deny Russia membership in the WTO. But it had been clear long before the first shots were fired in the Caucasus that Russia had no hope or desire of joining the WTO anyway—at least, not without securing a whole series of concessions to Moscow's demands. And the WTO states have failed to resolve their disagreements during trade negotiations on admitting Russia.

The Doha Round negotiations, the ongoing effort by WTO member states to achieve greater liberalization in global trade, broke down in July 2008. The East European states are unable to reach agreement with the West European countries, and Western Europe is at loggerheads with the US over agricultural subsidies. Washington's plan to create a free-trade zone in South America has been rejected, while Venezuelan President Hugo Chavez's Bolivarian Alternative for the Americas (ALBA) is attracting the support of governments that have little in common with Chavez's radical policies.

What is going on?

As a rule, the global economy changes dramatically during times of heightened crisis. Over the last few years, we have seen a shift from free trade among countries with 'seamless' borders to a system dominated by fierce politicized competition and opposing economic blocs. In many ways, the situation today resembles Europe before the outbreak of World War I. This is not just another banal doomsday warning. The era of protectionism has arrived, and it has led to the political conflicts we are now witnessing.

True, Russia has no chance of joining the WTO now, but this has been the case for a long time.

True, Moscow's stock market is falling, but share prices started to drop long before the world had ever heard of South Ossetia. And true, this will hurt relations with the West, but were they so good before?

Most investors will invest in any country where they can turn a good profit, regardless of its political orientation. But as soon as investment returns take a dive, any sharp political crisis quickly becomes a compelling reason to pull out of the country.

As it turns out, President Medvedev, who had the reputation of being a liberal before he took the presidential oath, is now leading Russia's serious confrontation with the West. But we shouldn't blame Medvedev for this, because the fundamental reasons for the global crisis can be found in the inherent confrontational nature of capitalism.

WHAT'S NEXT?

Dramatic years of 'transition' that shocked and depressed Russian society were logically followed by popular apathy and a deep-seated need for stability, not only expressed in government propaganda but also shared by the great mass of people. By the end of the first decade of the twenty-first century, the situation was changing—the economy and public morale was recovering, though most of the contradictions and problems of the previous period remained unresolved. Moscow became a wealthy city, its real estate prices making London look cheap. Russian teams were winning all sorts of international competitions, filmmakers were presenting new movies with budgets more impressive than anywhere in Europe, and the new middle class was enjoying its long-dreamed-of consumerist prosperity. The currency was stable, the government seemed popular and the people full of hope.

Too good to be true. At least in Russia. And at least in the longer term.

After 17 years of change, capitalist Russia became a society dramatically different from its Soviet predecessor, and in many ways it can even look successful. But it has failed to develop a ruling elite that can legitimize itself in any positive way, except by reminding people about the past glory of the Empire or of the USSR. It has failed to unite society and to give it a new common cultural identity, not to mention a shared ideology. And all these problems will come to the fore when the economic crisis really starts hitting the country.

A society recovering from the traumas of the past decade has to enter a new period, when international crisis will bite, social conflicts become more visible and political tension will form the new public agenda. In fact, this is not so different from any other society in today's capitalist world.

At last, Russia is becoming a 'normal' country.